This journal belongs to

....

You are a beautiful woman of God,
precious to Him in every way.
As you seek Him, He will show you
the mysteries of life and unfold His unique
plans for you—a life full of rich blessings and delight.
Wherever your journey may take you, God is right
there with you. He is thinking of you and smiling down
on you. Let this journal inspire you to express your
thoughts, embrace your dreams, record your prayers,
and listen to what God is saying to you.

How precious are your thoughts about me, O God.
They cannot be numbered!

PSALM 139:17 NLT

WHEN GOD
THINKS OF YOU

He Smiles

PROMISE JOURNAL

Ellie Claire™
gift & paper expressions

...inspired by life...

Special Plans

This is the real gift: you have been given
the breath of life, designed with a unique, one-of-a-kind soul
that exists forever—the way that you choose to live it
doesn't change the fact that you've been given the gift of
being now and forever. Priceless in value,
you are handcrafted by God, who has a personal design
and plan for each of us.

"gift of life"

May God's love guide you through
the special plans He has for your life.

"unique"

Allow your dreams a place in your prayers and plans.
God-given dreams can help you move
into the future He is preparing for you.

"Priceless"

Lift up your eyes. Your heavenly Father waits to bless you—
in inconceivable ways to make your life what
you never dreamed it could be.

ANNE ORTLUND

"one of a kind"

God created us with an overwhelming desire to soar....
He designed us to be tremendously productive and
"to mount up with wings like eagles," realistically dreaming
of what He can do with our potential.

CAROL KENT

"personal design"

"Handcrafted by God"

Dec 28, 2014   Special Plans

Today the sermon was about Resolutions — whatever we are doing for God — we can always do more.

I want to do more bible study & more time drawing closer to God. I am so thankful for the opportunity to Teach the Adult Ladies class in Sunday School. This year I want to do even more as we study together. I want to inspire these women to study even more in depth. Some have already let me know they are listening to their Bible on CD that I was able to give them for Christmas.

I am so excited & pleased to get to play with the Perry Co Dulcimer Club. Today we played at the Nursing Home & we sang for James Hamblin. Finally we got to give to him after He has given so much through his life. Lord please be with them & his family

The LORD will work out his plans for my life—
for your faithful love, O LORD, endures forever.

PSALM 138:8 NLT

Day #1 of eating healthy.

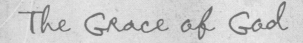

The Grace of God

But God, being <u>rich in mercy</u>, because of His great <u>love</u>
with which He loved us, even when we were dead
in our transgressions, made us alive together with Christ
(by grace you have been saved), and raised us up
with Him, and seated us with Him in the heavenly places
in Christ Jesus, so that in the ages to come He might show
the surpassing riches of His grace in kindness toward us in
Christ Jesus. For by grace you have been saved
through faith; and that not of yourselves, it is the <u>gift</u>
<u>of God</u>; not as a result of works, so that no one may boast.
For we are <u>His</u> workmanship, <u>created in Christ Jesus</u>
<u>for good works</u>, which God prepared beforehand
so that we would walk in them.

EPHESIANS 2:4–10 NASB

My grace is sufficient for thee:
for my strength is made perfect in weakness.

2 CORINTHIANS 12:9 KJV

For of His fullness we have all received,
and grace upon grace.

JOHN 1:16 NASB

December 29, 2014

Only 2 more days before we move to the new clinic. We were very busy today, working on the Peds side with Marti + her student Ashley.

After work I met Mom, Robin + Shelly at Circle T for supper, then mommy + Robin came by the house to hear the dulcimer. I'm very pleased with the sound + looks, it is very nice.

I read my testimony to them. I still have some work to do on it before I record it on line for Tell Your Story.com. A way to reach many people over the internet with your personal testimony.

Day 2 eating better

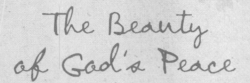

The Beauty of God's Peace

In comparison with this big world, the human heart
is only a small thing. Though the world is so large,
it is utterly unable to satisfy this tiny heart.
Our ever growing soul and its capacities can be satisfied
only in the infinite God. As water is restless until
it reaches its level, so the soul has no peace
until it rests in God.

SADHU SUNDAR SINGH

Peace is a margin of power around our daily need.
Peace is a consciousness of springs too deep
for earthly droughts to dry up.

HARRY EMERSON FOSDICK

Drop Thy still dews of quietness
till all our strivings cease;
take from our souls the strain and stress,
and let our ordered lives confess
the beauty of Thy peace.

JOHN GREENLEAF WHITTIER

Be still, and know that I am God.

PSALM 46:10 KJV

Wonderful Love

Show me the wonder of your great love.... Keep me as the
apple of your eye; hide me in the shadow of your wings.

Give thanks to the LORD, for he is good!
His faithful love endures forever.

PSALM 136:1 NLT

The LORD is gracious and compassionate,
slow to anger and rich in love.
The LORD is good to all;
he has compassion on all he has made....
Your kingdom is an everlasting kingdom,
and your dominion endures through all generations.
The LORD is trustworthy in all he promises
and faithful in all he does.

PSALM 145:8–9, 13 NIV

Don't be afraid, I've redeemed you. I've called your name.
You're mine. When you're in over your head, I'll be there
with you. When you're in rough waters, you will not go down.
When you're between a rock and a hard place,
it won't be a dead end—because I am God,
your personal God, the Holy of Israel, your Savior.
I paid a huge price for you...! *That's* how much
you mean to me! *That's* how much I love you!

ISAIAH 43:1–4 MSG

*Every one of us as human beings is known
and loved by the Creator apart
from every other human on earth.*

JAMES DOBSON

Countless Beauties

May God give you eyes to see beauty
only the heart can understand.

From the world we see, hear, and touch, we behold
inspired visions that reveal God's glory. In the sun's light,
we catch warm rays of grace and glimpse His eternal design.
In the birds' song, we hear His voice and it reawakens
our desire for Him. At the wind's touch, we feel
His Spirit and sense our eternal existence.

All the world is an utterance of the Almighty.
Its countless beauties, its exquisite adaptations,
all speak to you of Him.

PHILLIPS BROOKS

The longer I live, the more my mind dwells upon
the beauty and the wonder of the world.

JOHN BURROUGHS

You are God's created beauty and the focus
of His affection and delight.

JANET L. SMITH

Those who dwell, as scientists or laymen, among the beauties
and mysteries of the earth are never alone or weary of life....
Those who contemplate the beauty of the earth find reserves
of strength that will endure as long as life lasts.

RACHEL CARSON

He has made everything beautiful in its time.

ECCLESIASTES 3:11 NIV

The Blessing of the Lord

The LORD bless thee, and keep thee: the LORD make his face
shine upon thee, and be gracious unto thee: the LORD lift up his
countenance upon thee, and give thee peace.

NUMBERS 6:24–26 KJV

Praise be to the God and Father of our Lord Jesus Christ,
who has blessed us in the heavenly realms
with every spiritual blessing in Christ.

EPHESIANS 1:3 NIV

May it please you to bless the house of your servant,
so that it may continue forever before you. For you
have spoken, and when you grant a blessing to your servant,
O Sovereign LORD, it is an eternal blessing!

2 SAMUEL 7:29 NLT

Blessed are those who hunger
and thirst for righteousness,
for they shall be satisfied.

MATTHEW 5:6 NASB

Blessed are the merciful: for they shall obtain mercy.
Blessed are the pure in heart: for they shall see God.
Blessed are the peacemakers:
for they shall be called the children of God.

MATTHEW 5:7–9 KJV

God bless you and utterly satisfy your heart...with Himself.

AMY CARMICHAEL

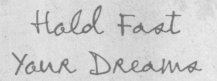

Hold Fast Your Dreams

Hold fast your dreams!
Within your heart
Keep one still, secret spot
Where dreams may go
And, sheltered so,
May thrive and grow...
O keep a place apart,
Within your heart,
For little dreams to go!

LOUISE DRISCOLL

Always stay connected to people
and seek out things that bring you joy.
Dream with abandon. Pray confidently.

BARBARA JOHNSON

The human heart has hidden treasures,
In secret kept, in silence sealed;—
The thoughts, the hopes, the dreams, the pleasures,
Whose charms were broken if revealed.

CHARLOTTE BRONTE

....

....

....

....

....

....

....

....

....

....

....

....

....

....

....

....

....

....

....

*Hope deferred makes the heart sick,
but when desire comes, it is a tree of life.*

PROVERBS 13:12 NLT

God-Provision

Steep yourself in God-reality, God-initiative, God-provisions.
You'll find all your everyday human concerns will be met.
Don't be afraid of missing out. You're my dearest friends!
The Father wants to give you the very kingdom itself.

LUKE 12:29 MSG

Let your gentleness be evident to all.
The Lord is near. Do not be anxious about anything,
but in every situation, by prayer and petition,
with thanksgiving, present your requests to God.

PHILIPPIANS 4:5–6 NIV

I am like a luxuriant fruit tree.
Everything you need is to be found in me.

HOSEA 14:8 MSG

And God is able to bless you abundantly,
so that in all things at all times, having all that you need,
you will abound in every good work.

2 CORINTHIANS 9:8 NIV

Your Father knows that you need these things.
But seek His kingdom, and these things will be added
to you. Do not be afraid, little flock, for your Father
has chosen gladly to give you the kingdom.

LUKE 12:30–32 NASB

*At the very heart of the universe
is God's desire to give and to forgive.*

The Goodness of God

The goodness of God is infinitely more wonderful
than we will ever be able to comprehend.

A. W. TOZER

All that is good, all that is true, all that is beautiful,
all that is beneficent, be it great or small, be it perfect
or fragmentary, natural as well as supernatural,
moral as well as material, comes from God.

CARDINAL JOHN HENRY NEWMAN

God's love is like a river springing up in the Divine Substance
and flowing endlessly through His creation,
filling all things with life and goodness and strength.

THOMAS MERTON

We walk without fear, full of hope and courage
and strength to do His will, waiting for the endless good
which He is always giving as fast as He can
get us able to take it in.

GEORGE MACDONALD

Savor little glimpses of God's goodness and His majesty,
thankful for the gift of them.

_____

_____

_____

_____

_____

_____

_____

_____

_____

_____

_____

_____

_____

_____

_____

_____

Open your mouth and taste, open your eyes and see—how good GOD is.
Blessed are you who run to him. Worship GOD if you want the best;
worship opens doors to all his goodness.

PSALM 34:8–9 MSG

The Lord's Favor

May the favor of the Lord our God rest upon us;
establish the work of our hands for us—
yes, establish the work of our hands.

PSALM 90:17 NIV

I will bless my people and their homes....
I will send the showers they need.
There will be showers of blessing.

EZEKIEL 34:26 NLT

Praise the LORD, my soul;
all my inmost being, praise his holy name.
Praise the LORD, my soul,
and forget not all his benefits—
who forgives all your sins
and heals all your diseases,
who redeems your life from the pit
and crowns you with love and compassion,
who satisfies your desires with good things
so that your youth is renewed like the eagle's.

PSALM 103:1–5 NIV

....

....

....

....

....

....

....

....

....

....

....

....

....

....

There is plenitude in God.... God is a vast reservoir of blessing who supplies us abundantly.

EUGENE PETERSON

Child of God

When we call on God, He bends down His ear to listen,
as a father bends down to listen to his little child.

ELIZABETH CHARLES

He only is the Maker
of all things near and far;
He paints the wayside flower,
He lights the evening star;
the wind and waves obey Him,
by Him the birds are fed;
much more to us, His children,
He gives our daily bread.

MATTHIAS CLAUDIUS

Remember you are very special to God
as His precious child. He has promised to complete
the good work He has begun in you. As you continue
to grow in Him, He will make you a blessing to others.

God's children who joyously know and claim
who they are and whose they are will be most likely
to manifest the family likeness, just because
they know they are His children.

ALICE CHAPIN

What marvelous love the Father has extended to us!
Just look at it—we're called children of God!

1 JOHN 3:1 MSG

Love One Another

Watch what God does, and then you do it,
like children who learn proper behavior from their parents.
Mostly what God does is love you. Keep company with him
and learn a life of love. Observe how Christ loved us.
His love was not cautious but extravagant. He didn't love
in order to get something from us but to give
everything of himself to us. Love like that.

EPHESIANS 5:1–2 MSG

I pray that your love will overflow more and more,
and that you will keep on growing
in your knowledge and understanding.

PHILIPPIANS 1:9 NLT

Dear friends, since God so loved us, we also ought
to love one another.... If we love one another,
God lives in us and his love is made complete in us.

1 JOHN 4:11–12 NIV

A new command I give you:
Love one another. As I have loved you,
so you must love one another.

JOHN 13:34 NIV

....

....

....

....

....

....

....

....

....

....

....

....

....

....

Open your hearts to the love God instills....
God loves you tenderly. What He gives you is not
to be kept under lock and key, but to be shared.

MOTHER TERESA

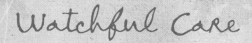

Watchful Care

He paints the lily of the field,
Perfumes each lily bell;
If He so loves the little flowers,
I know He loves me well.

MARIA STRAUS

God cares for the world He created, from the
rising of a nation to the falling of the sparrow.
Everything in the world lies under the watchful gaze
of His providential eyes, from the numbering of
the days of our life to the numbering of the hairs
on our head. When we look at the world
from that perspective, it produces within us
a response of reverence.

KEN GIRE

God's in His heaven—
All's right with the world!

ROBERT BROWNING

Beneath God's watchful eye
His saints securely dwell;
That Hand which bears all nature up
Shall guard His children well.

WILLIAM COWPER

*For He will give His angels charge concerning you,
to guard you in all your ways.*

PSALM 91:11 NASB

Wonderful Joy

So be truly glad! There is wonderful joy ahead....
You love him even though you have never seen him.
Though you do not see him now, you trust him;
and you rejoice with a glorious, inexpressible joy.

1 Peter 1:6, 8 nlt

Those the Lord has rescued will return. They will
enter Zion with singing; everlasting joy will crown their
heads. Gladness and joy will overtake them, and sorrow
and sighing will flee away.

Isaiah 35:10 niv

Rejoice evermore.

1 Thessalonians 5:16 kjv

You'll go out in joy, you'll be led into a whole
and complete life. The mountains and hills will lead
the parade, bursting with song. All the trees of the forest
will join the procession, exuberant with applause.

Isaiah 55:12 msg

You make known to me the path of life;
you will fill me with joy in your presence,
with eternal pleasures at your right hand.

Psalm 16:11 niv

He will once again fill your mouth
with laughter and your lips with shouts of joy.

Job 8:21 nlt

Through all eternity to Thee a joyful song I'll raise;
for oh! eternity's too short to utter all Thy praise.

JOSEPH ADDISON

In His Image

God's designs regarding you, and His methods of bringing
about these designs, are infinitely wise.

MADAME JEANNE GUYON

The God of the universe—the One who created everything
and holds it all in His hand—created each of us in His image,
to bear His likeness, His imprint. It is only when Christ
dwells within our hearts, radiating the pure light of His love
through our humanity, that we discover who we are
and what we were intended to be.

Stand outside this evening. Look at the stars. Know that you
are special and loved by the One who created them.

All that we have and are is one of the unique
and never-to-be repeated ways God has chosen to express
Himself in space and time. Each of us, made in His image
and likeness, is yet another promise He has made to the
universe that He will continue to love it and care for it.

BRENNAN MANNING

Made in His image, we can have real meaning,
and we can have real knowledge through
what He has communicated to us.

FRANCIS SCHAEFFER

So God created human beings in his own image.
In the image of God he created them;
male and female he created them.

God's Care

The LORD is my shepherd;
I have all that I need.
He lets me rest in green meadows;
he leads me beside peaceful streams.
He renews my strength.
He guides me along right paths,
bringing honor to his name.
Even when I walk
through the darkest valley,
I will not be afraid,
for you are close beside me.
Your rod and your staff
protect and comfort me.
You prepare a feast for me
in the presence of my enemies.
You honor me by anointing my head with oil.
My cup overflows with blessings.
Surely your goodness and unfailing love will pursue me
all the days of my life,
and I will live in the house of the LORD
forever.

PSALM 23:1–6 NLT

Give your entire attention to what God is doing right now,
and don't get worked up about what may or may not
happen tomorrow. God will help you deal with
whatever hard things come up when the time comes.

MATTHEW 6:34 MSG

God never abandons anyone on whom
He has set His love; nor does Christ,
the good shepherd, ever lose track of His sheep.

J. I. PACKER

A Life Transformed

To pray is to change. This is a great grace. How good of God
to provide a path whereby our lives can be taken over by love
and joy and peace and patience and kindness and goodness
and faithfulness and gentleness and self-control.

RICHARD J. FOSTER

You, too, can be changed for the better. Therein lies our
hope.... We are disciples in clay. And there is still the skill of
the Potter.

PETER MARSHALL

For God is, indeed, a wonderful Father who longs
to pour out His mercy upon us, and whose majesty is so great
that He can transform us from deep within.

TERESA OF AVILA

A life transformed by the power of God
is always a marvel and a miracle.

GERALDINE NICHOLAS

May our lives be illumined
by the steady radiance
renewed daily,
of a wonder,
the source of which
is beyond reason.

DAG HAMMARSKJÖLD

*Create in me a clean heart, O God;
and renew a right spirit within me.*

PSALM 51:10 KJV

The Majesty of God

Lord, our Lord,
how majestic is your name in all the earth!
You have set your glory in the heavens.
Through the praise of children and infants
you have established a stronghold against your enemies,
to silence the foe and the avenger.
When I consider your heavens,
the work of your fingers,
the moon and the stars,
which you have set in place,
what is mankind that you are mindful of them,
human beings that you care for them?
You have made them a little lower than the angels
and crowned them with glory and honor....
Lord, our Lord, how majestic is your name in all the earth!

PSALM 8:1–5, 9 NIV

Yours, O Lord, is the greatness and the power
and the glory and the victory and the majesty,
indeed everything that is in the heavens and the earth;
Yours is the dominion, O Lord, and You
exalt Yourself as head over all.

1 CHRONICLES 29:11 NASB

Where God is, there is heaven—heaven!
Where His Majesty reigns in glory.

TERESA OF AVILA

A Work of Art

Each one of us is God's special work of art.
Through us, He teaches and inspires, delights and
encourages, informs and uplifts all those who view our lives.
God, the master artist, is most concerned
about expressing Himself—His thoughts and His intentions—
through what He paints in our character....
[He] wants to paint a beautiful portrait of His Son in
and through your life. A painting like no other in all of time.

JONI EARECKSON TADA

Whether we are poets or parents or teachers
or artists or gardeners, we must start where we are
and use what we have. In the process of creation
and relationship, what seems mundane and trivial
may show itself to be holy, precious, part of a pattern.

LUCI SHAW

The artist, the novelist, the surgeon, the plumber,
the secretary, the lawyer, the homemaker, the farmer,
the teacher—all are praying by offering their work up to God.

RICHARD J. FOSTER

I *will give thanks to You, for I am fearfully and wonderfully made; wonderful are Your works.*

PSALM 139:14 NASB

God's Ways

For my thoughts are not your thoughts, neither are your ways
my ways, saith the LORD. For as the heavens are higher than
the earth, so are my ways higher than your ways, and my
thoughts than your thoughts.

ISAIAH 55:8–9 KJV

We have not ceased to pray for you and to ask
that you may be filled with the knowledge of His will
in all spiritual wisdom and understanding,
so that you will walk in a manner worthy of the Lord,
to please Him in all respects, bearing fruit in every
good work and increasing in the knowledge of God;
strengthened with all power, according to
His glorious might, for the attaining of all steadfastness
and patience; joyously giving thanks to the Father,
who has qualified us to share in the inheritance
of the saints in Light.

COLOSSIANS 1:9–12 NASB

O the depth of the riches both of the wisdom
and knowledge of God!
how unsearchable are his judgments,
and his ways past finding out! For who hath
known the mind of the Lord?
or who hath been his counsellor?

ROMANS 11:33–34 KJV

*In both simple and eloquent ways,
our infinite God personally reveals
glimpses of Himself in the finite.*

Enfolded in Peace

I will let God's peace infuse every part of today.
As the chaos swirls and life's demands pull at me
on all sides, I will breathe in God's peace that
surpasses all understanding. He has promised that
He would set within me a peace too deeply planted to be
affected by unexpected or exhausting demands.

Calm me, O Lord, as you stilled the storm,
Still me, O Lord, keep me from harm.
Let all the tumult within me cease,
Enfold me, Lord, in your peace.

CELTIC TRADITIONAL

God cannot give us a happiness and peace
apart from Himself, because it is not there.
There is no such thing.

C. S. LEWIS

I have been away and come back again many times
to this place. Each time I approach, I regret ever having left.
There is a peace here, a serenity, even before I enter.
Just the idea of returning becomes a balm for the wounds
I've collected elsewhere. Before I can finish even one knock,
the door opens wide and I am in His presence.

BARBARA FARMER

God's peace...exceeds anything we can understand.
His peace will guard your hearts and minds
as you live in Christ Jesus.

Restoration

The Spirit of the Sovereign LORD is on me,
because the LORD has anointed me
to proclaim good news to the poor.
He has sent me to bind up the brokenhearted,
to proclaim freedom for the captives
and release from darkness for the prisoners,
to proclaim the year of the LORD's favor
and the day of vengeance of our God,
to comfort all who mourn,
and provide for those who grieve in Zion—
to bestow on them a crown of beauty instead of ashes,
the oil of joy instead of mourning,
and a garment of praise
instead of a spirit of despair.
They will be called oaks of righteousness,
a planting of the LORD for the display of his splendor.

ISAIAH 61:1–3 NIV

The God of all grace, who called you
to his eternal glory in Christ, after you have
suffered a little while, will himself restore you
and make you strong, firm and steadfast.

1 PETER 5:10 NIV

The Lord promises to bind up the brokenhearted,
to give relief and full deliverance to those
whose spirits have been weighed down.

Unique Gifts

God has a wonderful plan for each person He has chosen. He
knew even before He created this world
what beauty He would bring forth from our lives.

LOUISE B. WYLY

Everyone has a unique role to fill in the world
and is important in some respect. Everyone, including
and perhaps especially you, is indispensable.

NATHANIEL HAWTHORNE

God gives us all gifts, special abilities that we
are entrusted with developing to help
serve Him and serve others.

He calls us by grace to perform our own unique function
within the Body of Christ. Then, again by grace,
He gives to each of us the spiritual gifts necessary to
fulfill our calling. As we serve Him, He makes that service
acceptable to Himself by grace, and then rewards us
a hundredfold by grace.

JERRY BRIDGES

This bright, new day, complete with twenty-four hours
of opportunities, choices, and attitudes,
comes with a perfectly matched set of 1,440 minutes.
This unique gift, this one day, cannot be exchanged,
replaced, or refunded. Handle with care. Make the most of it.
There is only one to a customer!

---

*God has given each of you a gift from his
great variety of spiritual gifts.
Use them well to serve one another.*

1 PETER 4:10 NLT

Designed on Purpose

It's in Christ that we find out who we are
and what we are living for. Long before we first
heard of Christ and got our hopes up, he had his eye on us,
had designs on us for glorious living, part of the overall
purpose he is working out in everything and everyone.

EPHESIANS 1:11–12 MSG

To every thing there is a season, and a time
to every purpose under the heaven.

ECCLESIASTES 3:1 KJV

It's not important who does the planting,
or who does the watering. What's important is that God
makes the seed grow. The one who plants and
the one who waters work together with the same purpose.
And both will be rewarded for their own hard work.
For we are both God's workers. And you are God's field.
You are God's building.

1 CORINTHIANS 3:7–9 NLT

All the days ordained for me were written in your book
before one of them came to be.

PSALM 139:16 NIV

The patterns of our days are always rearranging...
and each design for living is unique,
graced with its own special beauty.

God Hears

No matter where we are,
God can hear us from there!

Because we are His children, God hears our [requests].
The king of creation gives special heed
to the voice of His family. He is not only willing to hear us,
He loves to hear us.

MAX LUCADO

God doesn't need us to shout. We can whisper
and He still hears our prayers.

GARY SMALLEY AND JOHN TRENT

And then a little laughing prayer
Came running up the sky,
Above the golden gutters, where
The sorry prayers go by.
It had no fear of anything,
But in that holy place
It found the very throne of God
And smiled up in His face.

AMY CARMICHAEL

God hears and answers.... His ear is
ever open to the cry of His children.

E. M. BOUNDS

....

....

....

....

....

....

....

....

....

....

....

....

....

....

....

....

Because of Christ and our faith in him,
we can now come boldly and confidently into God's presence.

EPHESIANS 3:12 NLT

Trust His Love

Look at the birds of the air, that they do not sow,
nor reap nor gather into barns, and yet your heavenly Father
feeds them. Are you not worth much more than they?
And who of you by being worried can add a single hour
to his life? And why are you worried about clothing?
Observe how the lilies of the field grow; they do not toil
nor do they spin, yet I say to you that not even
Solomon in all his glory clothed himself
like one of these. But if God so clothes the grass
of the field, which is alive today and tomorrow
is thrown into the furnace, will He not much more
clothe you? You of little faith! Do not worry then, saying,
"What will we eat?" or "What will we drink?" or
"What will we wear for clothing?" For...your heavenly Father
knows that you need all these things. But seek first
His kingdom and His righteousness,
and all these things will be added to you.

MATTHEW 6:26–33 NASB

Trust the past to the mercy of God,
the present to His love, and the future to His Providence.

Sought and Found

It is God's will that we believe that we see Him continually,
though it seems to us that the sight be only partial; and
through this belief He makes us always to gain more grace,
for God wishes to be seen, and He wishes to be sought, and
He wishes to be expected, and He wishes to be trusted.

JULIAN OF NORWICH

A Christian is not one who is seeking God's favor and
forgiveness—he is one who has found them.

T. ROLAND PHILIPS

To seek God means first of all
to let yourself be found by Him.

God's nature is given me. His love is jealous for my life.
All His attributes are woven into the pattern of my spirit.
What a God is this! His life implanted in every child.
Thank You, Father, for this.

JIM ELLIOT

The person who has met God is not looking for something—
she has found it; she is not searching for light—
upon her the Light has already shined.

A. W. TOZER

I have sought Thy nearness;
With all my heart have I called Thee,
And going out to meet Thee
I found Thee coming toward me.

YEHUDA HALEVI

*If...you seek the L*ORD *your God, you will
find him if you seek him with all your heart
and with all your soul.*

Rest in Him

The promise of "arrival" and "rest" is still there
for God's people. God Himself is at rest.
And at the end of the journey we'll surely
rest with God. So let's keep at it and eventually
arrive at the place of rest.

HEBREWS 4:9–11 MSG

Come unto me, all ye that labour and are heavy laden, and I
will give you rest. Take my yoke upon you, and learn of me;
for I am meek and lowly in heart: and ye shall find rest unto
your souls. For my yoke is easy, and my burden is light.

MATTHEW 11:28–30 KJV

My soul finds rest in God alone; my salvation
comes from him. Truly he is my rock and my salvation;
he is my fortress, I will never be shaken....
My salvation and my honor depend on God;
he is my mighty rock, my refuge. Trust in him at all times,
you people; pour out your hearts to him,
for God is our refuge.

PSALM 62:1–2, 7–8 NIV

Rest in the LORD, and wait patiently for him.

PSALM 37:7 KJV

....

....

....

....

....

....

....

....

....

....

....

....

....

....

....

*When God finds a soul that rests in Him
and is not easily moved...to this same soul
He gives the joy of His presence.*

CATHERINE OF GENOA

Fresh Insights

With God, life is eternal—both in quality and length.
There is no joy comparable to the joy of discovering
something new from God, about God. If the continuing life
is a life of joy, we will go on discovering, learning.

EUGENIA PRICE

This life is not all. It is an "unfinished symphony"...
with those who know that they are related to God
and have felt the power of an endless life.

HENRY WARD BEECHER

Every day we live is a priceless gift of God, loaded with
possibilities to learn something new, to gain fresh insights.

DALE EVANS ROGERS

Face your deficiencies and acknowledge them....
Let them teach you patience, sweetness, insight.
When we do the best we can, we never know what miracle is
wrought in our life, or in the life of another.

HELEN KELLER

So let us know, let us press on to know the Lord....
He will come to us like the rain,
like the spring rain watering the earth.

Protection

The LORD is my light and my salvation—
whom shall I fear?
The LORD is the stronghold of my life—
of whom shall I be afraid?
One thing I ask from the LORD,
this only do I seek:
that I may dwell in the house of the LORD
all the days of my life,
to gaze on the beauty of the LORD
and to seek him in his temple.
For in the day of trouble
he will keep me safe in his dwelling;
he will hide me in the shelter of his sacred tent
and set me high upon a rock.

PSALM 27:1, 4–5 NIV

The LORD says, "I will rescue those who love me.
I will protect those who trust in my name.
When they call on me, I will answer;
I will be with them in trouble.
I will rescue and honor them.
I will reward them with a long life
and give them my salvation."

PSALM 91:14–16 NLT

....

....

....

....

....

....

....

....

....

....

....

....

....

....

....

....

Leave behind your fear and dwell
on the lovingkindness of God—
that you may recover by gazing on Him.

Treasure in Nature

If we are children of God, we have a tremendous
treasure in nature and will realize that it is holy and sacred.
We will see God reaching out to us in every wind that blows,
every sunrise and sunset, every cloud in the sky,
every flower that blooms, and every leaf that fades.

OSWALD CHAMBERS

He made you so you could share in His creation,
could love and laugh and know Him.

TED GRIFFEN

Look up at all the stars in the night sky and
hear your Father saying, "I carefully set each one in its place.
Know that I love you more than these." Sit by the lake's edge,
listening to the water lapping the shore, and hear your Father
gently calling you to that place near His heart.

You are a creation of God unequaled anywhere
in the universe.... Thank Him for yourself and then
for all the rest of His glorious handiwork.

NORMAN VINCENT PEALE

....

....

....

....

....

....

....

....

....

....

....

....

....

....

....

....

....

The heavens declare the glory of God;
the skies proclaim the work of his hands.

PSALM 19:1 NIV

Good Plans

Remember the things I have done in the past. For I alone
am God! I am God, and there is none like me. Only I can tell
you the future before it even happens. Everything I plan will
come to pass, for I do whatever I wish.

ISAIAH 46:9–10 NLT

"For I know the plans I have for you," declares the LORD,
"plans to prosper you and not to harm you,
plans to give you hope and a future."

JEREMIAH 29:11 NIV

Commit to the LORD whatever you do,
and he will establish your plans.

PROVERBS 16:3 NIV

The LORD will work out his plans for my life—
for your faithful love, O LORD, endures forever.
Don't abandon me, for you made me.

PSALM 138:8 NLT

No eye has seen, no ear has heard,
and no mind has imagined
what God has prepared for those who love him.

1 CORINTHIANS 2:9 NLT

*Every person's life is a fairy tale
written by God's fingers.*

HANS CHRISTIAN ANDERSEN

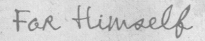

For Himself

Although it be good to think upon the kindness of God,
and to love Him and worship Him for it; yet it is
far better to gaze upon the pure essence of Him
and to love Him and worship Him for Himself.

The reason for loving God is God Himself, and the measure
in which we should love Him is to love Him without measure.

BERNARD OF CLAIRVAUX

We desire many things, and God offers us only one thing.
He can offer us only one thing—Himself.
He has nothing else to give. There is nothing else to give.

PETER KREEFT

Joy is perfect acquiescence in God's will because
the soul delights itself in God Himself.

H. W. WEBB-PEPLOE

We are of such value to God that He came to live among us...
and to guide us home. He will go to any length to seek us,
even to being lifted high upon the cross to draw us back to
Himself. We can only respond by loving God for His love.

CATHERINE OF SIENA

....

....

....

....

....

....

....

....

....

....

....

....

....

....

....

....

The LORD alone shall be exalted.

ISAIAH 2:11 KJV

Full Protection

But let all who take refuge in you be glad;
let them ever sing for joy. Spread your protection over them,
that those who love your name may rejoice in you.
Surely, Lord, you bless the righteous;
you surround them with your favor as with a shield.

PSALM 5:11–12 NIV

By my power I will make my people strong,
and by my authority they will go wherever they wish.
I, the Lord, have spoken!

ZECHARIAH 10:12 NLT

I am with you and will keep you wherever you go.

GENESIS 28:15 NASB

How great is the goodness you have stored up for those
who fear you. You lavish it on those who come to you for
protection, blessing them before the watching world.

PSALM 31:19 NLT

If God be for us, who can be against us?

ROMANS 8:31 KJV

Though I am surrounded by troubles,
you will protect me from the anger of my enemies.
You reach out your hand,
and the power of your right hand saves me.

PSALM 138:7 NLT

*God is steadfast as your rock,
faithful as your protector,
sleepless as your watcher.*

Eternal Hope

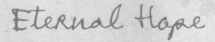

Hope floods my heart with delight!
Running on air, mad with life, dizzy, reeling,
Upward I mount—faith is sight, life is feeling....
I am immortal! I know it! I feel it!

MARGARET WITTER FULLER

Hope sees the invisible, feels the intangible,
and achieves the impossible.

Life is what we are alive to. It is not length but breadth....
Be alive to...goodness, kindness, purity, love, history, poetry,
music, flowers, stars, God, and eternal hope.

MALTBIE D. BABCOCK

Faith, as the Bible defines it, is present-tense action.
Faith means being sure of what we hope for...now.

JONI EARECKSON TADA

Do you not know that day follows night,
that flood comes after ebb, that spring and summer
succeed winter? Have hope then! Always have hope!
God fails you not.

CHARLES H. SPURGEON

I *pray that the eyes of your heart may be enlightened
in order that you may know the hope to which he has called you.*

God Is Our Refuge

Hear my cry, O God;
Give heed to my prayer.
From the end of the earth I call to You
when my heart is faint;
Lead me to the rock that is higher than I.
For You have been a refuge for me,
A tower of strength against the enemy.
Let me dwell in Your tent forever;
Let me take refuge in the shelter of Your wings.

PSALM 61:1–4 NASB

God is our refuge and strength,
always ready to help in times of trouble.
So we will not fear when earthquakes come
and the mountains crumble into the sea.

PSALM 46:1–2 NLT

Whom have I in heaven but You?
And besides You, I desire nothing on earth.
My flesh and my heart may fail,
But God is the strength of my heart
and my portion forever....
But as for me, the nearness of God is my good;
I have made the Lord GOD my refuge,
That I may tell of all Your works.

PSALM 73:25–26, 28 NASB

When God has become...our refuge and our fortress,
then we can reach out to Him in the midst of a broken world
and feel at home while still on the way.

HENRI J. M. NOUWEN

Overflowing Praise

All enjoyment spontaneously overflows into praise....
The world rings with praise...walkers praising
the countryside, players praising their favorite game....
I think we delight to praise what we enjoy because
the praise not merely expresses but completes the enjoyment;
it is the appointed consummation.

C. S. LEWIS

God's pursuit of praise from us and our pursuit of pleasure
in Him are one and the same pursuit. God's quest to be
glorified and our quest to be satisfied reach their goal in this
one experience: our delight in God which overflows in praise.

JOHN PIPER

Earth, with her thousand voices, praises God.

SAMUEL TAYLOR COLERIDGE

Praise God from whom all blessings flow;
Praise Him, all creatures here below;
Praise Him above, ye heav'nly host:
Praise Father, Son, and Holy Ghost.

DOXOLOGY

May your life become one of glad and unending praise
to the Lord as you journey through this world.

TERESA OF AVILA

O sing unto the LORD a new song:
sing unto the LORD, all the earth.

PSALM 96:1 KJV

Love Never Fails

If I speak with the tongues of men and of angels,
but do not have love, I have become a noisy gong
or a clanging cymbal. If I have the gift of prophecy,
and know all mysteries and all knowledge;
and if I have all faith, so as to remove mountains,
but do not have love, I am nothing. And if I give
all my possessions to feed the poor, and if I
surrender my body to be burned, but do not have love,
it profits me nothing. Love is patient, love is kind and
is not jealous; love does not brag and is not arrogant,
does not act unbecomingly; it does not seek its own,
is not provoked, does not take into account a wrong suffered,
does not rejoice in unrighteousness, but rejoices
with the truth; bears all things, believes all things,
hopes all things, endures all things. Love never fails.

1 CORINTHIANS 13:1–8 NASB

Examine me, GOD...
Make sure I'm fit inside and out
So I never lose sight of your love,
But keep in step with you, never missing a beat.

PSALM 26:2–3 MSG

God is the sunshine that warms us, the rain that melts the frost and waters the young plants. The presence of God is a climate of strong and bracing love, always there.

JOAN ARNOLD

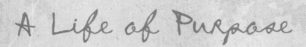

A Life of Purpose

Happiness is living by inner purpose, not by outer pressures.

DAVID AUGSBURGER

I believe that nothing that happens to me is meaningless,
and that it is good for us all that it should be so,
even if it runs counter to our own wishes. As I see it,
I'm here for some purpose, and I only hope I may fulfill it.

DIETRICH BONHOEFFER

Singleness of purpose is one of the chief essentials for
success in life, no matter what may be one's aim.

JOHN D. ROCKEFELLER JR.

The meaning of earthly existence lies,
not as we have grown used to thinking, in prospering,
but in the development of the soul.

ALEKSANDR SOLZHENITSYN

The purpose of life is a life of purpose.

ROBERT BYRNE

This is the true joy in life: the being used for a purpose
recognized by yourself as a mighty one.

GEORGE BERNARD SHAW

And we know that all things work together for good
to them that love God, to them who are
the called according to his purpose.

ROMANS 8:28 KJV

Abundant Life

I came so they can have real and eternal life,
more and better life than they ever dreamed of.

JOHN 10:10 MSG

In the beginning was the Word, and the Word was with God,
and the Word was God. He was in the beginning with God.
All things came into being through Him, and apart from
Him nothing came into being that has come into being.
In Him was life, and the life was the Light of men.

JOHN 1:1–4 NASB

Be glad, people of Zion,
rejoice in the LORD your God,
for he has given you the autumn rains
because he is faithful.
He sends you abundant showers,
both autumn and spring rains

JOEL 2:23 NIV

As for you, see that what you have heard from the beginning
remains in you. If it does, you also will remain in the Son and
in the Father. And this is what he promised us—eternal life.

1 JOHN 2:24–25 NIV

....

....

....

....

....

....

....

....

....

....

....

....

....

....

....

....

....

*He is looking for people who will come
in simple dependence upon His grace....
At this very moment, He's looking at you.*

JACK HAYFORD

Happiness and Gratitude

It is not how much we have, but how much we enjoy,
that makes happiness.

CHARLES H. SPURGEON

Sometimes our thoughts turn back toward a corner
in a forest, or the end of a bank, or an orchard
powdered with flowers, seen but a single time...
yet remaining in our hearts and leaving in soul and body
an unappeased desire which is not to be forgotten,
a feeling we have just rubbed elbows with happiness.

GUY DE MAUPASSANT

The joy of receiving is in far more than the gifts—that when
we receive graciously and gladly, we reciprocate the gift with
joy and gratitude; and in that moment of shared happiness
and understanding, giver and receiver "connect."

JENNY WALTON

Our inner happiness depends not
on what we experience but on the degree of
our gratitude to God, whatever the experience.

ALBERT SCHWEITZER

I would maintain that thanks are the highest form of
thought, and that gratitude is happiness doubled by wonder.

G. K. CHESTERTON

The Word of God

For as the rain cometh down, and the snow from heaven,
and returneth not thither, but watereth the earth,
and maketh it bring forth and bud, that it may give
seed to the sower, and bread to the eater: so shall my word
be that goeth forth out of my mouth: it shall not return
unto me void, but it shall accomplish that which I please,
and it shall prosper in the thing whereto I sent it.

ISAIAH 55:10–11 KJV

Not one word has failed of all His good promise.

1 KINGS 8:56 NASB

For the word of the LORD holds true,
and we can trust everything he does.
He loves whatever is just and good;
the unfailing love of the LORD fills the earth.
The LORD merely spoke,
and the heavens were created.
He breathed the word,
and all the stars were born.
He assigned the sea its boundaries
and locked the oceans in vast reservoirs.

PSALM 33:4–7 NLT

God is the God of promise. He keeps His word,
even when that seems impossible.

COLIN URQUHART

His Beautiful World

The God who holds the whole world in His hands
wraps Himself in the splendor of the sun's light
and walks among the clouds.

Forbid that I should walk through
Thy beautiful world with unseeing eyes:
Forbid that the lure of the market-place
should ever entirely steal my heart away from the love
of the open acres and the green trees:
Forbid that under the low roof of workshop or office
or study I should ever forget Thy great overarching sky.

JOHN BAILLIE

Our Creator would never have made such lovely days,
and given us the deep hearts to enjoy them,
above and beyond all thought,
unless we were meant to be immortal.

NATHANIEL HAWTHORNE

All the flowers God has made are beautiful.
The rose in its glory and the lily in its whiteness
do not rob the tiny violet of its sweet smell,
or the daisy of its charming simplicity.

ST. THÉRÈSE OF LISIEUX

The whole earth is full of his glory.

ISAIAH 6:3 KJV

God's Peace

The tender mercy of our God, with which the Sunrise
from on high will visit us, [will] shine upon those who
sit in darkness...to guide our feet into the way of peace.

LUKE 1:78–79 NASB

May God give you more and more mercy, peace, and love.

JUDE 1:2 NLT

Now in Christ Jesus you who formerly were far off
have been brought near by the blood of Christ.
For He Himself is our peace.

EPHESIANS 2:13–14 NASB

Grace, mercy and peace from God the Father
and from Jesus Christ, the Father's Son,
will be with us in truth and love.

2 JOHN 1:3 NIV

Peace be with you, dear brothers and sisters,
and may God the Father and the Lord Jesus Christ
give you love with faithfulness. May God's grace
be eternally upon all who love our Lord Jesus Christ.

EPHESIANS 6:23–24 NLT

Now the God of hope fill you
with all joy and peace in believing.

ROMANS 15:13 KJV

$\mathcal{W}$here there is peace, God is.

GEORGE HERBERT

Completely Loved

What good news! God knows me completely
and still loves me.

You are valuable just because you exist. Not because of what
you do or what you have done, but simply because you are.
Just think about the way Jesus honors you...and smile.

MAX LUCADO

There is nothing we can do that will make God
love us less, and there's nothing we can do that will
make Him love us more. He will always and forever
love us unconditionally. What He wants from us is
that we love Him back with all our heart.

God, who is love—who is, if I may say it this way,
made out of love—simply cannot help
but shed blessing on blessing upon us.

HANNAH WHITALL SMITH

We love him, because he first loved us.

1 JOHN 4:19 KJV

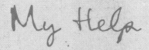

My Help

I will lift up mine eyes unto the hills,
from whence cometh my help. My help cometh
from the Lord, which made heaven and earth.
He will not suffer thy foot to be moved:
he that keepeth thee will not slumber. Behold, he that
keepeth Israel shall neither slumber nor sleep.
The Lord is thy keeper: the Lord is thy shade upon
thy right hand. The sun shall not smite thee by day,
nor the moon by night. The Lord shall preserve thee
from all evil: he shall preserve thy soul. The Lord shall
preserve thy going out and thy coming in from
this time forth, and even for evermore.

PSALM 121:1–8 KJV

Let us then approach God's throne of grace
with confidence, so that we may receive mercy and find grace
to help us in our time of need.

HEBREWS 4:16 NIV

$\mathcal{W}_e$ *have a Father in heaven who is almighty, who loves His children*
as He loves His only-begotten Son, and whose very joy and delight it is to...
help them at all times and under all circumstances.

GEORGE MÜELLER

Made for Joy

Our hearts were made for joy. Our hearts were made
to enjoy the One who created them. Too deeply planted
to be much affected by the ups and downs of life,
this joy is a knowing and a being known by our Creator.
He sets our hearts alight with radiant joy.

Joy is the touch of God's finger. The object of our longing
is not the touch but the Toucher. This is true of all good
things—they are all God's touch. Whatever we desire,
we are really desiring God.

PETER KREEFT

If one is joyful, it means that one is faithfully
living for God, and that nothing else counts;
and if one gives joy to others one is doing God's work.
With joy without and joy within, all is well.

JANET ERSKINE STUART

Joy is the echo of God's life within us.

Live for today but hold your hands open to tomorrow.
Anticipate the future and its changes with joy.
There is a seed of God's love in every event,
every circumstance, every unpleasant situation
in which you may find yourself.

BARBARA JOHNSON

The joy of the Lord is your strength.

Contentment

I have learned to be content in whatever circumstances I am.
I know how to get along with humble means, and I also know
how to live in prosperity; in any and every circumstance I
have learned the secret of being filled and going hungry,
both of having abundance and suffering need.
I can do all things through Him who strengthens me.

PHILIPPIANS 4:11–13 NASB

Be content with who you are, and don't put on airs.
God's strong hand is on you; he'll promote you
at the right time. Live carefree before God;
he is most careful with you.

I PETER 5:6–7 MSG

Godliness with contentment is great gain.
For we brought nothing into the world,
and we can take nothing out of it. But if we have food
and clothing, we will be content with that.

I TIMOTHY 6:6–8 NIV

You're blessed when you're content with just who you are—
no more, no less. That's the moment you find yourselves
proud owners of everything that can't be bought.

MATTHEW 5:5 MSG

Contentment is not the fulfillment of what you want,
but the realization of how much you already have.

Nothing But Grace

There is nothing but God's grace.
We walk upon it; we breathe it; we live and die by it;
it makes the nails and axles of the universe.

ROBERT LOUIS STEVENSON

Grace is no stationary thing, it is ever becoming.
It is flowing straight out of God's heart.
Grace does nothing but re-form and convey God.
Grace makes the soul conformable to the will of God.
God, the ground of the soul, and grace go together.

MEISTER ECKHART

Grace and gratitude belong together like heaven and earth.
Grace evokes gratitude like the voice an echo.
Gratitude follows grace as thunder follows lightning.

KARL BARTH

To be grateful is to recognize the Love of God in
everything He has given us—and He has given us everything.
Every breath we draw is a gift of His love,
every moment of existence is a gift of grace,
for it brings with it immense graces from Him.

THOMAS MERTON

*God is sheer mercy and grace; not easily angered,
he's rich in love.... As far as sunrise is from sunset,
he has separated us from our sins.*

PSALM 103:8, 12 MSG

Faith

Now faith is confidence in what we hope for
and assurance about what we do not see....
By faith we understand that the universe was formed
at God's command, so that what is seen was not made out of
what was visible.... And without faith it is impossible
to please God, because anyone who comes to him
must believe that he exists and that he rewards
those who earnestly seek him.

HEBREWS 11:1, 3, 6 NIV

By entering through faith into what God has always
wanted to do for us—set us right with him,
make us fit for him—we have it all together with God
because of our Master Jesus. And that's not all:
We throw open our doors to God and discover
at the same moment that he has already
thrown open his door to us.
We find ourselves standing where we always hoped
we might stand—out in the wide open spaces
of God's grace and glory, standing tall
and shouting our praise.

ROMANS 5:1–2 MSG

Faith...*means knowing something is real, this moment, all around you, even when you don't see it. Great faith isn't the ability to believe long and far into the misty future. It's simply taking God at His word and taking the next step.*

JONI EARECKSON TADA

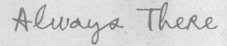

Always There

We need never shout across the spaces to an absent God.
He is nearer than our own soul,
closer than our most secret thoughts.

A. W. Tozer

God is always present in the temple of your heart...His home.
And when you come in to meet Him there, you find that it is
the one place of deep satisfaction where every longing is met.

Always be in a state of expectancy, and see that you leave
room for God to come in as He likes.

Oswald Chambers

God's hand is always there; once you grasp it
you'll never want to let it go.

The Lord doesn't always remove the sources of stress in our
lives...but He's always there and cares for us.
We can feel His arms around us on the darkest night.

Dr. James Dobson

....
....
....
....
....
....
....
....
....
....
....
....
....
....
....
....
....
....
....
....
....

How lovely are Your dwelling places, O LORD of hosts!
My soul longed and even yearned for the courts of the LORD;
my heart and my flesh sing for joy to the living God....
For a day in Your courts is better than a thousand outside.

PSALM 84:1–2, 10 NASB

Made Complete

But thanks be to God, who always leads us as captives in
Christ's triumphal procession and uses us to spread the
aroma of the knowledge of him everywhere. For we are to
God the pleasing aroma of Christ among those who are
being saved and those who are perishing.

2 CORINTHIANS 2:14–15 NIV

For in Him all the fullness of Deity dwells in bodily form,
and in Him you have been made complete.

COLOSSIANS 2:9–10 NASB

Yet you, LORD, are our Father.
We are the clay, you are the potter;
we are all the work of your hand.

ISAIAH 64:8 NIV

For God, who said, "Let light shine out of darkness,"
made his light shine in our hearts to give us the light of the
knowledge of God's glory displayed in the face of Christ.
But we have this treasure in jars of clay to show that this
all-surpassing power is from God and not from us.

2 CORINTHIANS 4:6–7 NIV

*Lord, help me to spread Your fragrance everywhere I go,
and may Your radiant light be visible through me.*

Endless Wonders

Little drops of water,
Little grains of sand,
Make the mighty ocean
And the pleasant land.
Little deeds of kindness,
Little words of love,
Help to make earth happy
Like the heaven above.

JULIA FLETCHER CARNEY

As we grow in our capacities to see and enjoy the joys
that God has placed in our lives, life becomes a glorious
experience of discovering His endless wonders.

God moves in a mysterious way
His wonders to perform;
He plants His footsteps in the sea,
And rides upon the storm.

WILLIAM COWPER

Dear Lord, grant me the grace of wonder. Surprise me,
amaze me, awe me in every crevice of Your universe....
Each day enrapture me with your marvelous things
without number. I do not ask to see the reason for it all;
I ask only to share the wonder of it all.

JOSHUA ABRAHAM HESCHEL

I *will show wonders in the heavens and on the earth.*

Free to Live

GOD, your God, will cut away the thick calluses on your heart
and your children's hearts, freeing you to love GOD,
your God, with your whole heart and soul and live,
really live.... And you will make a new start,
listening obediently to GOD, keeping all his commandments
that I'm commanding you today. GOD, your God, will outdo
himself in making things go well for you.... Love GOD,
your God. Walk in his ways. Keep his commandments,
regulations, and rules so that you will live, really live,
live exuberantly, blessed by GOD.... Oh yes, he is life itself.

DEUTERONOMY 30:6–9, 16, 20 MSG

This is what I have observed to be good:
that it is appropriate for a person to eat, to drink
and to find satisfaction in their toilsome labor under the sun
during the few days of life God has given them—
for this is their lot. Moreover, when God gives someone
wealth and possessions, and the ability to enjoy them,
to accept their lot and be happy in their toil—
this is a gift of God. They seldom reflect on
the days of their life, because God keeps them
occupied with gladness of heart.

ECCLESIASTES 5:18–20 NIV

I asked God for all things that I might enjoy life.
He gave me life that I might enjoy all things.

Someone Special

The Creator thinks enough of you to have sent Someone
very special so that you might have life—
abundantly, joyfully, completely, and victoriously.

When we love someone, we want to be with them,
and we view their love for us with great honor even
if they are not a person of great status. For this reason—
and not because of our great status—God values our love.
So much, in fact, that He suffered greatly on our behalf.

JOHN CHRYSOSTOM

One of Jesus' specialties is to
make somebodies out of nobodies.

HENRIETTA MEARS

We have missed the full impact of the Gospel if we have
not discovered what it is to be ourselves, loved by God,
irreplaceable in His sight, unique among our fellow men.

BRUCE LARSON

This is the real gift: we have been given the breath of life,
designed with a unique, one-of-a-kind soul that exists
forever.... Priceless in value, we are handcrafted by God,
who has a personal design and plan for each of us.

WENDY MOORE

....

....

....

....

....

....

....

....

....

....

....

....

....

....

....

....

God demonstrates His own love toward us,
in that while we were yet sinners, Christ died for us.

ROMANS 5:8 NASB

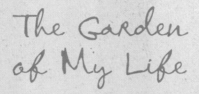

The Garden of My Life

At that same time, a fine vineyard will appear.
There's something to sing about! I, God, tend it.
I keep it well-watered. I keep careful watch over it so that
no one can damage it.... Even if it gives me thistles
and thornbushes, I'll just pull them out and burn them up.
Let that vine cling to me for safety, let it find a good and
whole life with me, let it hold on for a good and whole life.

ISAIAH 27:2–5 MSG

Abide in Me, and I in you. As the branch
cannot bear fruit of itself unless it abides in the vine,
so neither can you unless you abide in Me.
I am the vine, you are the branches;
he who abides in Me and I in him, he bears much fruit,
for apart from Me you can do nothing.

JOHN 15:4–5 NASB

....

....

....

....

....

....

....

....

....

....

....

....

....

....

....

*It is God's knowledge of me, His careful husbanding
of the ground of my being, His constant presence in the garden
of my little life that guarantees my joy.*

W. PHILLIP KELLER

Refreshing Solitude

Solitude liberates us from entanglements by
carving out a space from which we can see ourselves
and our situation before the Audience of One.
Solitude provides the private place where we can
take our bearings and so make God our North Star.

OS GUINNESS

Settle yourself in solitude and you will
come upon Him in yourself.

TERESA OF AVILA

We must drink deeply from the very Source, the deep calm
and peace of interior quietude and refreshment of God,
allowing the pure water of divine grace to flow plentifully
and unceasingly from the Source itself.

MOTHER TERESA

I will refresh the weary and satisfy the faint.

JEREMIAH 31:25 NIV

At times it is only necessary to rest one's self
in silence for a few minutes, in order to take off
the pressure and become wonderfully refreshed.

HORATIO WILLIS DRESSER

*Whoever drinks of the water that I will give him shall never thirst;
but the water that I will give him will become in him
a well of water springing up to eternal life.*

JOHN 4:13–14 NASB

Of Great Value

Are not five sparrows sold for two pennies?
Yet not one of them is forgotten by God. Indeed,
the very hairs of your head are all numbered. Don't be afraid;
you are worth more than many sparrows.

LUKE 12:6–7 NIV

For God bought you with a high price.
So you must honor God with your body.

1 CORINTHIANS 6:20 NLT

The Spirit himself testifies with our spirit that we
are God's children. Now if we are children,
then we are heirs—heirs of God and co-heirs with Christ,
if indeed we share in his sufferings in order
that we may also share in his glory.

ROMANS 8:16–17 NIV

As your life was highly valued in my sight this day,
so may my life be highly valued in the sight of the LORD,
and may He deliver me from all distress.

1 SAMUEL 26:24 NASB

For you know that it was not with perishable things such as
silver or gold that you were redeemed...but with the precious
blood of Christ, a lamb without blemish or defect.

1 PETER 1:18–19 NIV

*You are in the Beloved...therefore infinitely dear to the Father,
unspeakably precious to Him.*

Norman F. Dowty

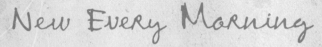

New Every Morning

Morning has broken like the first morning,
Blackbird has spoken like the first bird....
Praise with elation, praise every morning,
God's re-creation of the new day!

ELEANOR FARJEON

Always new. Always exciting. Always full of promise.
The mornings of our lives, each a personal daily miracle!

GLORIA GAITHER

If you have time to open the back door in the morning
while you're drinking your coffee and look at the sky or hear
the chorus the birds offer, you have time for the marvelous.
You may only have a moment before the polite chaos of the
day starts, but that moment can stretch to the horizon....
Most of life is fascinating if looked at closely enough.

DIANE ACKERMAN

That is God's call to us—simply to be people who
are content to live close to Him and to renew
the kind of life in which the closeness is felt and experienced.

THOMAS MERTON

··

··

··

··

··

··

··

··

··

··

··

··

··

··

··

··

··

··

··

··

··

··

The faithful love of the Lord never ends! His mercies never cease.
Great is his faithfulness; his mercies begin afresh each morning.

LAMENTATIONS 3:22–23 NLT

Mighty Prayer

Our Father which art in heaven, hallowed be thy name.
Thy kingdom come, thy will be done in earth,
as it is in heaven. Give us this day our daily bread.
And forgive us our debts, as we forgive our debtors.
And lead us not into temptation, but deliver us from evil:
for thine is the kingdom, and the power,
and the glory, for ever. Amen.

MATTHEW 6:9–13 KJV

I fall to my knees and pray to the Father,
the Creator of everything in heaven and on earth.
I pray that from his glorious, unlimited resources he will
empower you with inner strength through his Spirit.
Then Christ will make his home in your hearts as you
trust in him. Your roots will grow down into God's love
and keep you strong. And may you have the power to
understand, as all God's people should, how wide,
how long, how high, and how deep his love is.
May you experience the love of Christ, though it is too great
to understand fully. Then you will be made complete with
all the fullness of life and power that comes from God.
Now all glory to God, who is able, through his mighty power
at work within us, to accomplish infinitely more than
we might ask or think. Glory to him in the church
and in Christ Jesus through all generations forever and ever!
Amen.

EPHESIANS 3:14–21 NLT

They who seek the throne of grace find that throne in every place;
If we live a life of prayer, God is present everywhere.

OLIVER HOLDEN

Special Gifts

Every person ever created is so special that their presence in
the world makes it richer and fuller and more wonderful than
it could ever have been without them.

We were not sent into this world to do anything
into which we cannot put our hearts.

JOHN RUSKIN

Use what talents you possess:
the woods would be very silent
if no birds sang there
except those that sang best.

HENRY VAN DYKE

God gives everyone a special gift
and a special place to use it.

You have a unique message to deliver, a unique song to sing,
a unique act of love to bestow. This message,
this song, and this act of love have been
entrusted exclusively to the one and only you.

JOHN POWELL, S.J.

Live your life while you have it. Life is a splendid gift—
there is nothing small about it.

FLORENCE NIGHTINGALE

God has given each of you
a gift from his great variety of spiritual gifts.
Use them well to serve one another.

1 PETER 4:10 NLT

Song of Praise

"Behold, God is my salvation, I will trust and not be afraid;
for the LORD GOD is my strength and song, and He has
become my salvation." Therefore you will joyously draw
water from the springs of salvation.

ISAIAH 12:2–3 NASB

The LORD is my strength and my defense;
he has become my salvation.
He is my God, and I will praise him,
my father's God, and I will exalt him....
Who is like you—majestic in holiness,
awesome in glory, working wonders?

EXODUS 15:2, 11 NIV

Then I heard something like the voice of a great multitude
and like the sound of many waters and like the sound of
mighty peals of thunder, saying, "Hallelujah! For the Lord
our God, the Almighty, reigns. Let us rejoice
and be glad and give the glory to Him."

REVELATION 19:6–7 NASB

I will give thanks to the LORD with all my heart;
I will tell of all Your wonders. I will be glad and exult in You;
I will sing praise to Your name, O Most High.

PSALM 9:1–2 NASB

Since God is Lord of heaven and earth,
how can I keep from singing?

By Love Alone

By love alone is God enjoyed; by love alone delighted in,
by love alone approached and admired.
His nature requires love.

THOMAS TRAHERNE

In the very beginning it was God who formed us
by His Word. He made us in His own image. God was spirit
and He gave us a spirit so that He could come into us
and mingle His own life with our life.

MADAME JEANNE GUYON

You who have received so much love share it with others.
Love others the way that God has loved you, with tenderness.

MOTHER TERESA

Love does not allow lovers
to belong anymore to themselves,
but they belong only to the Beloved.

DIONYSIUS

There is an essential connection between experiencing God,
loving God, and trusting God. You will trust God only as
much as you love Him, and you will love Him to the extent
you have touched Him, rather that He has touched you.

BRENNAN MANNING

*Love the LORD your God with all your heart,
all your soul, and all your strength.*

DEUTERONOMY 6:5 NLT

Seek the Lord

The God who made the world and everything in it is the
Lord of heaven and earth...: He himself gives all men life
and breath and everything else.... God did this so that men
would seek him and perhaps reach out for him and find him,
though he is not far from each one of us. "For in him we live,
and move, and have our being."

ACTS 17:24–28 NIV

I love those who love me; and those
who diligently seek me will find me.

PROVERBS 8:17 NASB

The LORD is good to those whose hope is in him,
to the one who seeks him;
it is good to wait quietly
for the salvation of the LORD.

LAMENTATIONS 3:25–26 NIV

Those who know your name trust in you,
for you, O LORD, do not abandon those who search for you.

PSALM 9:10 NLT

*God is not an elusive dream or a phantom to chase,
but a divine person to know. He does not avoid us, but seeks us.
When we seek Him, the contact is instantaneous.*

NEVA COYLE

Destiny

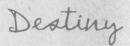

Recognizing who we are in Christ and aligning our life
with God's purpose for us gives a sense of destiny....
It gives form and direction to our life.

JEAN FLEMING

When we live life centered around what others like, feel,
and say, we lose touch with our own identity.
I am an eternal being, created by God. I am
an individual with purpose. It's not what I get from life,
but who I am, that makes the difference.

NEVA COYLE

When God made space and worlds that move in space,
and clothed our world with air, and gave us such eyes and
such imaginations as those we have, He knew what
the sky would mean to us.... We cannot be certain that
this was not indeed one of the chief purposes
for which nature was created.

C. S. LEWIS

God has a purpose for your life
and no one else can take your place.

May the favor of the Lord our God rest upon us;
establish the work of our hands for us.

Paths of Life

The path of the righteous is like the light of dawn,
that shines brighter and brighter until the full day.

PROVERBS 4:18 NASB

You have made known to me the paths of life;
you will fill me with joy in your presence.

ACTS 2:28 NIV

Trust in the LORD with all your heart
and lean not on your own understanding;
in all your ways submit to him,
and he will make your paths straight.

PROVERBS 3:5–6 NIV

Thy word is a lamp unto my feet,
and a light unto my path.

PSALM 119:105 KJV

I will lead blind Israel down a new path,
guiding them along an unfamiliar way.
I will brighten the darkness before them
and smooth out the road ahead of them.

ISAIAH 42:16 NLT

Come, and let us go up to the mountain of the LORD...
and he will teach us of his ways,
and we will walk in his paths.

MICAH 4:2 KJV

The best things are nearest...light in your eyes,
flowers at your feet, duties at your hand,
the path of God just before you.

ROBERT LOUIS STEVENSON

God Listens

You can talk to God because God listens. Your voice
matters in heaven. He takes you very seriously.
When you enter His presence, the attendants turn to you
to hear your voice. No need to fear that you will be ignored.
Even if you stammer or stumble, even if what you have to say
impresses no one, it impresses God—and He listens.

MAX LUCADO

Open wide the windows of our spirits and fill us full of light;
open wide the door of our hearts, that we may receive and
entertain Thee with all our powers of adoration.

CHRISTINA ROSSETTI

Whoever walks toward God one step,
God runs toward him two.

We come this morning—
Like empty pitchers to a full fountain,
With no merits of our own,
O Lord—open up a window of heaven...
And listen this morning.

JAMES WELDON JOHNSON

God listens in compassion and love,
just like we do when our children come to us.
He delights in our presence.

RICHARD J. FOSTER

....

....

....

....

....

....

....

....

....

....

....

....

....

....

....

....

....

I love the Lord because he hears my voice and my prayer for mercy.
Because he bends down to listen, I will pray as long as I have breath!

PSALM 116:1–2 NLT

Delight in the Lord

Take delight in the LORD, and he will give you
the desires of your heart. Commit your way to the LORD;
trust in him and he will do this: He will make your
righteous reward shine like the dawn,
your vindication like the noonday sun.

PSALM 37:4–6 NIV

I delight to do thy will, O my God.

PSALM 40:8 KJV

Send me your light and your faithful care, let them lead me;
let them bring me to your holy mountain, to the place
where you dwell. Then will I go to the altar of God,
to God, my joy and my delight.

PSALM 43:3–4 NIV

I will thank the LORD with all my heart
as I meet with his godly people.
How amazing are the deeds of the LORD!
All who delight in him should ponder them.
Everything he does reveals his glory and majesty.
His righteousness never fails.
He causes us to remember his wonderful works.
How gracious and merciful is our LORD!

PSALM 111:1–4 NLT

....

....

....

....

....

....

....

....

....

....

....

....

....

....

....

....

....

....

....

*Our fulfillment comes in knowing God's glory,
loving Him for it, and delighting in it.*

Shining Through

Don't ever let yourself get so busy that you
miss those little but important extras in life—
the beauty of a day...the smile of a friend...the serenity
of a quiet moment alone. For it is often life's smallest
pleasures and gentlest joys that make the biggest
and most lasting difference.

Dear Lord...shine through me, and be so in me
that every soul I come in contact with may feel
Your presence in my soul.... Let me thus praise You
in the way You love best, by shining on those around me.

JOHN HENRY NEWMAN

Someone said to me once that we can
see the features of God in a single smile.
Look for that smile in the people you meet.

CHRISTOPHER DE VINCK

Let Jesus be in your heart,
Eternity in your spirit,
The world under your feet,
The will of God in your actions.
And let the love of God shine forth from you.

CATHERINE OF GENOA

*We are transfigured much like the Messiah,
our lives gradually becoming brighter and more beautiful
as God enters our lives and we become like him.*

2 CORINTHIANS 3:18 MSG

Holy and Whole

May God himself, the God who makes everything
holy and whole, make you holy and whole, put you together—
spirit, soul, and body—and keep you fit for the coming
of our Master, Jesus Christ. The One who called you
is completely dependable.

1 THESSALONIANS 5:23–24 MSG

Everything of God finds its proper place in him
without crowding. Not only that, but all the broken and
dislocated pieces of the universe—people and things,
animals and atoms—get properly fixed and fit together
in vibrant harmonies, all because of his death.

COLOSSIANS 1:19–20 MSG

Great is the LORD, and most worthy of praise,
in the city of our God, his holy mountain.
Beautiful in its loftiness, the joy of the whole earth....
For this God is our God for ever and ever;
he will be our guide even to the end.

PSALM 48:1–2, 14 NIV

*God's fingers can touch nothing
but to mold it into loveliness.*

GEORGE MACDONALD

Totally Aware

God is every moment totally aware of each one of us.
Totally aware in intense concentration and love....
No one passes through any area of life, happy or tragic,
without the attention of God with him.

EUGENIA PRICE

God promises to keep us in the palm of [His] hand, with or
without our awareness. God has already made a space for us,
even if we have not made a space for God.

DAVID AND BARBARA SORENSEN

The "air" which our souls need also envelops all of us
at all times and on all sides. God is round about us...
on every hand, with many-sided and all-sufficient grace.

OLE HALLESBY

Because God is responsible for our welfare,
we are told to cast all our care upon Him, for He cares for us.
God says, "I'll take the burden—don't give it a thought—
leave it to Me." God is keenly aware that we are
dependent upon Him for life's necessities.

BILLY GRAHAM

God reads the secrets of the heart.
God reads its most intimate feelings,
even those which we are not aware of.

JEAN-NICHOLAS GROU

Casting all your care upon him;
for he careth for you.

1 PETER 5:7 KJV

The Love of God

Who shall separate us from the love of Christ?
Shall trouble or hardship or persecution or famine or
nakedness or danger or sword?... No, in all these things
we are more than conquerors through him who loved us.
For I am convinced that neither death nor life,
neither angels nor demons, neither the present
nor the future, nor any powers, neither height nor depth,
nor anything else in all creation, will be able to separate us
from the love of God that is in Christ Jesus our Lord.

ROMANS 8:35, 37–39 NIV

We know how much God loves us, and we have
put our trust in his love. God is love, and all who live in love
live in God, and God lives in them.

1 JOHN 4:16 NLT

One thing God has spoken, two things have I heard:
"Power belongs to you, God,
and with you, Lord, is unfailing love."

PSALM 62:11–12 NIV

Keep yourselves in God's love as you wait
for the mercy of our Lord Jesus Christ
to bring you to eternal life.

JUDE 1:21 NIV

....

....

....

....

....

....

....

....

....

....

....

....

....

....

....

....

Nothing can separate you from His love, absolutely nothing....
God is enough for time, and God is enough for eternity. God is enough!

HANNAH WHITALL SMITH

Every Need

God wants nothing from us except our needs,
and these furnish Him with room to display His bounty
when He supplies them freely.... Not what I have,
but what I do not have, is the first point of contact
between my soul and God.

CHARLES H. SPURGEON

Jesus Christ has brought every need, every joy,
every gratitude, every hope of ours before God.
He accompanies us and brings us into the presence of God.

DIETRICH BONHOEFFER

Do not dwell upon your inner failings.... Just do this:
Bring your soul to the Great Physician—exactly as you are,
even and especially at your worst moment....
For it is in such moments that you will
most readily sense His healing presence.

TERESA OF AVILA

If you have a special need today, focus your full attention
on the goodness and greatness of your Father rather
than on the size of your need. Your need is so small
compared to His ability to meet it.

My God shall supply all your need
according to his riches in glory by Christ Jesus.

PHILIPPIANS 4:19 KJV

Lavish Gift-Giving

Long before he laid down earth's foundations,
he had us in mind, had settled on us as the focus of his love,
to be made whole and holy by his love. Long, long ago
he decided to adopt us into his family through Jesus Christ.
(What pleasure he took in planning this!) He wanted us
to enter into the celebration of his lavish gift-giving
by the hand of his beloved Son.

EPHESIANS 1:4–6 MSG

If you sinful people know how to give good gifts
to your children, how much more will your heavenly Father
give good gifts to those who ask him.

MATTHEW 7:11 NLT

Be filled with the Spirit, speaking to one another
with psalms, hymns, and songs from the Spirit.
Sing and make music from your heart to the Lord,
always giving thanks to God the Father for everything,
in the name of our Lord Jesus Christ.

EPHESIANS 5:18–20 NIV

Isn't everything you have and
everything you are sheer gifts from God?

1 CORINTHIANS 4:7 MSG

Because of His boundless love, He became what we are in order that He might make us what He is.

IRENAEUS

The Sea
Remains the Sea

Dear Lord, today I thought of the words
of Vincent Van Gogh, "It is true that there is an ebb
and flow, but the sea remains the sea." You are the sea.
Although I may experience many ups and downs
in my emotions and often feel great shifts in my inner life,
You remain the same.... There are days of sadness and
days of joy; there are feelings of guilt and feelings
of gratitude; there are moments of failure and moments
of success; but all of them are embraced
by Your unwavering love. My only real temptation
is to doubt Your love...to remove myself from the
healing radiance of Your love. To do these things
is to move into the darkness of despair.
O Lord, sea of love and goodness, let me not fear
too much the storms and winds of my daily life,
and let me know that there is ebb and flow...
but that the sea remains the sea.
Amen.

HENRI J. M. NOUWEN

Do not be afraid to enter the cloud
that is settling down on your life. God is in it.
The other side is radiant with His glory.

L. B. COWMAN

....

....

....

....

....

....

....

....

....

....

....

....

....

....

....

....

....

You rule over the surging sea;
when its waves mount up, you still them.

PSALM 89:9 NIV

God Delights in You

The Lord your God is with you, the Mighty Warrior
who saves. He will take great delight in you;
in his love he will no longer rebuke you,
but will rejoice over you with singing.

ZEPHANIAH 3:17 NIV

I'll lead you to buried treasures,
secret caches of valuables—confirmations that it is,
in fact, I, God...who calls you by your name.

ISAIAH 45:3 MSG

The Lord directs the steps of the godly.
He delights in every detail of their lives.
Though they stumble, they will never fall,
for the Lord holds them by the hand.

PSALM 37:23–24 NLT

You'll get a brand-new name straight from the mouth of God.
You'll be a stunning crown in the palm of God's hand,
a jeweled gold cup held high in the hand of your God.
No more will anyone call you Rejected, and your country
will no more be called Ruined. You'll be called
Hephzibah (My Delight), and your land Beulah (Married),
because God delights in you.

ISAIAH 62:2–5 MSG

We are all precious in His sight.

Faithful Guide

God, who has led you safely on so far,
will lead you on to the end. Be altogether at rest in the
loving holy confidence which you ought to have
in His heavenly Providence.

FRANCIS DE SALES

Guidance is a sovereign act. Not merely does God
will to guide us by showing us His way...whatever mistakes
we may make, we shall come safely home. Slippings and
strayings there will be, no doubt, but the everlasting arms
are beneath us; we shall be caught, rescued, restored.
This is God's promise; this is how good He is.
And our self-distrust, while keeping us humble,
must not cloud the joy with which we lean on
our faithful, covenant God.

J. I. PACKER

I never cease to pray
that God will guard and keep you safe
within His love each day.
May you be guided by His word
In all you say and do.

JANIE HARPER FORD

We do not understand the intricate pattern
of the stars in their courses,
but we know that He who created them does,
and that just as surely as He guides them,
He is charting a safe course for us.

BILLY GRAHAM

All the paths of the LORD are lovingkindness and truth
To those who keep His covenant and His testimonies.

PSALM 25:10 NASB

Think on These Things

Whatsoever things are true, whatsoever things are honest,
whatsoever things are just, whatsoever things are pure,
whatsoever things are lovely, whatsoever things
are of good report; if there be any virtue,
and if there be any praise, think on these things.

PHILIPPIANS 4:8 KJV

Search me, God, and know my heart;
test me and know my anxious thoughts.
See if there is any offensive way in me,
and lead me in the way everlasting.

PSALM 139:23–24 NIV

The LORD is in his holy Temple; the LORD still rules
from heaven. He watches everything closely,
examining every person on earth....
For the righteous LORD loves justice.
The virtuous will see his face.

PSALM 11:4, 7 NLT

How precious also are Your thoughts to me, O God!
How vast is the sum of them!
If I should count them, they would outnumber the sand.
When I awake, I am still with You.

PSALM 139:17–18 NASB

The happiness of your life depends
upon the character of your thoughts.

Ellie Claire™ Gift & Paper Corp.
Minneapolis, MN 55337
www.ellieclaire.com

When God Thinks of You...He Smiles

Journal
© 2011 Ellie Claire Gift & Paper Corp.

ISBN 978-1-60936-237-9

Scripture references are from the following sources:
The Holy Bible, King James Version (KJV).
The Holy Bible, New International Version (NIV).
Copyright © 1973, 1978, 1984 by International Bible Society.
Used by permission of Zondervan Bible Publishers.
The New American Standard Bible® (NASB),
Copyright © 1960, 1962, 1963, 1968, 1971, 1972, 1973, 1975, 1977, 1995
by The Lockman Foundation. Used by permission.
The Holy Bible, New Living Translation (NLT), copyright 1996.
Used by permission of Tyndale House Publishers, Inc., Wheaton, Illinois 60189.
All rights reserved. The Message (MSG).
Copyright © 1994, 1994, 1995, 1996, 2000, 2001, 2002.
Used by permission of NavPress Publishing Group.

Excluding Scripture verses,
references to men and masculine pronouns
have been replaced with gender-neutral references.

Compiled by Joanie Garborg and Marilyn Jansen
Cover and interior design by Jeff and Lisa Franke

Printed in China.